New York as a British Colony

Jannell Khu

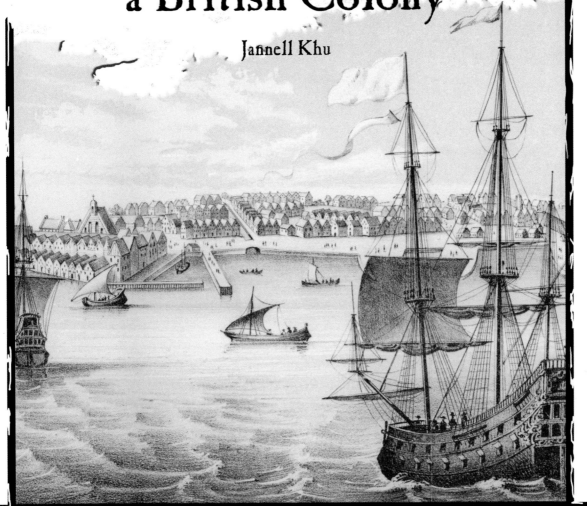

ROSEN CLASSROOM
PRIMARYSOURCE

Rosen Classroom Books & Materials

New York

Published in 2003 by The Rosen Publishing Group, Inc.
29 East 21st Street, New York, NY 10010

Book Design: Ron A. Churley

Photo Credits: Cover, pp. 1, 10 (inset), 18 © Bettmann/Corbis; pp. 4, 16 © The New-York Historical Society; pp. 4 (inset), 14 © Hulton/Archive; p. 6 © Art Resource; p. 8 © The Mariners' Museum/Corbis; p. 10 © Granger Collection; p. 12 © Corbis; p. 15 © Lee Snider; Lee Snider/Corbis; p. 20 © Francis G. Mayer/Corbis.

ISBN: 0-8239-8405-2
6-pack ISBN: 0-8239-8417-6

Manufactured in the United States of America

CPSIA Compliance Information: Batch #WR017070RC: For Further Information contact Rosen Publishing, New York, New York at 1-800-237-9932

Contents

Peter Stuyvesant

New World, New Netherland

Long before European settlers sailed across the Atlantic Ocean to the "New World," Native American groups like the **Algonquian** and **Iroquois** lived in the area that later became New York state. In 1609, an English explorer named Henry Hudson claimed much of that land for the Dutch merchants he worked for. The Dutch named the land New Netherland.

In 1624, Dutch settlers established a colony called Fort Orange near what is now the city of Albany. The Dutch traded with local Native Americans for furs, which sold for high prices in Europe. Soon, more Dutch colonists settled in New Amsterdam on the tip of Manhattan Island. In 1647, the Dutch sent a man named Peter Stuyvesant to be the fourth governor of New Netherland.

◀ Dutch settlers sailed up what is now the Hudson River to reach the colony at Fort Orange. The colonists probably saw many Native American villages like this one along the way. Native Americans sometimes lived in longhouses, like the ones shown in this picture. Native Americans built the longhouses by using young trees to make a frame, then covering the frame with bark.

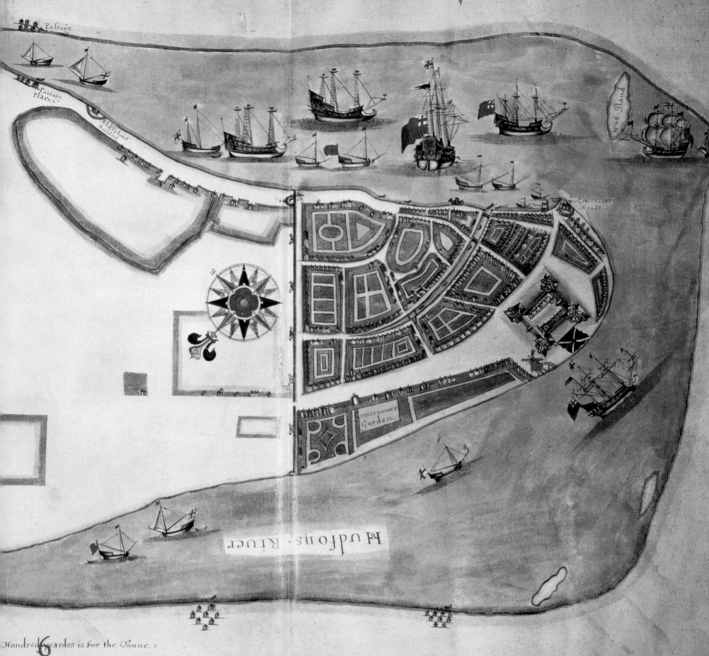

LONGE · ISLELAND

Passage

Passage PLACE

E

Governours Garden

Gouernours House

Hudsons River

THE · MAINE · LAND

Hundred yeardes is for the Towne

200   400   600   500

New York

In 1664, King Charles II of England decided to take over New Netherland. He wanted to control the **profitable** fur trade the Dutch had established with the Native Americans. The king's brother, James, duke of York, sent nearly 2,000 soldiers to New Amsterdam. The Dutch were outnumbered, and Peter Stuyvesant was forced to **surrender**. New Netherland was renamed New York in honor of James, and New Amsterdam became New York City. England now controlled most of the Atlantic coast of North America.

The Dutch were glad to be rid of Stuyvesant, who had been a stern leader. They welcomed British rule. The British government allowed the Dutch to work, worship, and live as they always had.

◀ This map of New Amsterdam was created in 1664. It was given to James, duke of York, after the English captured New Netherland from the Dutch. "Longe Isleland," or Long Island, can be seen at the top of the map. The Hudson River is called "Hudsons River" on this map. The artist painted many ships in the harbor to show that New Amsterdam was a busy and successful colony.

Colonists Learn from Native Americans

Native Americans showed the first settlers how to raise and prepare crops that grew well in the New York area, such as corn, beans, and squash. The early colonists shared this knowledge with each other and passed it down through their families. For many years, colonists used the Native American method of grinding corn in a bowl to make cornmeal for bread. The Native Americans also taught the colonists how to hunt and fish, and showed them which wild plants could be used as medicines.

◀ The Native Americans depended on fish for many of their meals. Fish were plentiful in the lakes and rivers of New York. The Native Americans showed the colonists the best ways to catch, clean, and cook fish. The artist who made this picture was named Theodor de Bry. He put his initials, T.B., at the bottom of the picture underneath the large log in the fire.

A
Brief Description
OF
NEW-YORK:
Formerly Called
New-Netherlands.
With the Places thereunto Adjoyning.

Together with the
Manner of its Scituation, Fertility of the Soyle,
Healthsulness of the Climate, and the
Commodities thence produced.

ALSO
Some Directions and Advice to such as shall go
thither: An Account of what Commodities they shall
take with them; The Profit and Pleasure that
may accrew to them thereby.

LIKEWISE
A Brief RELATION of the Customs of the
Indians there.

By DANIEL DENTON.

LONDON,
Printed for John Hancock, at the first Shop in Popes-Head-Aley in
Cornhil at the three Bibles, and William Bradley at the three Bibles
in the Minories. 1670.

King James II

English Governors

The first English governor of New York was a man named Richard Nicolls. He made sure the Dutch colonists were treated fairly. After Nicolls retired, the colonists chose their own leaders and made some of their own laws.

King Charles died in 1685. His brother, James, became King James II of England. James decided that he would make New York part of a larger colony called New England. He sent a man named Edmund Andros to govern the new colony. Andros took away the colonists' voting rights and told them they no longer owned the land.

The colonists of New York were angry that King James and the British government had taken away their rights. There were so many complaints that Andros was removed from power and sent back to England in 1689.

◄ This picture shows King James in the wig and fancy clothes that were fashionable at the English court. The small picture shows the first page from a booklet published in London in 1670. It is the one of the first descriptions of New York written after England took control of New Netherland from the Dutch.

Fighting over New York

By the late 1600s, both England and France had colonies in North America. The French had claimed land in what is now known as Canada and northern New York. Both countries wanted New York for its rich farmland, profitable trade routes, and **natural resources**.

In 1689, a series of wars broke out between England and France. The two countries fought for control of New York for almost seventy-five years! The last of these wars was from 1754 to 1763. It was called the French and Indian War because most of the Native Americans in the area fought on the side of the French.

◀ This map was created by the French in 1755 during the French and Indian War. It shows the English colonial territories in orange and some of the French colonial territories in green. The pink areas on the map are lands that both England and France wanted to claim.

1755			
	By Sum brought forward ...	411	16	1½
	By Cash to my Bro. John supposed to be as they were 5 dubloons ...	21	13	4
May 28	By a large Bay Horse of Saml. McRoberts ...	10	—	6
29	By Phurras for a Bell ...	—	5	9
	By Ditto gave ...	—	11	6
	By Ropes &c ...	—	5	—
June 1	By altering my Calese ...	—	1	3
2	By Captain Ormes Servant ...	—	1	3
3	By Cresaps pd. ...	2	16	10
7	By Mr. Shirley's Servant ...	—	1	3
8	By John Alton ...	—	10	—
	By making a black Stock ...	—	4	—
	By Cash gave to — ...	—	5	—
13	By Washing ...	—	10	9
	By Tho. Phurras ...	—	2	10½
17	By Col. Burton's Servant ...	—	2	10½
27	By Cleaning my Pistols ...	—	3	1½
July 2	By 8 days attendance of a Nurse in my Sickness ...	—	8	—
4	By Milk ...	—	5	9
	By 3 pair Hopples ...	—	9	7
21	By Mr. Hawthorn for a Mattrass ...	1	2	6½
22	By Washing ...	—	5	9
	By Thomas Phurras for a Horse ...	2	1	6
	By Joseph Bunnian - Batman ...	—	5	9
	By Smith for Shoeing my Horse ...	—	1	3
23	By Expences at McCrackens ...	—	5	9
24	By Jos. Oliver ...	—	6	4
	By Expences at Winchester ...	—	2	6
	By Ditto at Edward Thompson's ...	—	5	9
27	By Water Mellons ...	—	1	3
31	By 40 Bushels of Oats ...	2	—	—
Augt. 1	By Mr. Posey ...	4	6	8
	By my Brothers Serv. 1/3. By Besley inkd. Ford 96/3 ...	—	7	6
	By Mr. Dalton for Paying Bell. & Meads acct. ...	4	6	8
	By Sum carried Over	£466	12	3½

14

The French and Indian War in New York

During the French and Indian War, the Algonquian Native Americans fought for the French. Some of the Iroquois fought for the British. Many important battles of the French and Indian War were fought in New York.

In 1757, the French gained control of northern New York and the Hudson River. British forces fought hard to get this area back. The British attacked a French fort between Lake George and Lake Champlain. They

captured the fort and renamed it Fort Ticonderoga. In 1763, England won the war. France had to give up most of its land in North America.

◀ Many battles were fought at Fort Ticonderoga during the French and Indian War. This is a photograph of Fort Ticonderoga as it looks today.

◀ This is a page from General George Washington's account book, written during the French and Indian War. Washington fought on the side of the British.

New York Grows!

When the British took control of New York in 1664, about 9,000 people lived in the whole colony. New York City was a small seaport town. By 1771, just eight years after the end of the French and Indian War, the colony of New York was home to about 168,000 people!

Many New York colonists were farmers. Others built sawmills to cut lumber and shipyards to build boats. As New York City grew larger, people opened inns, shops, and markets. The city became an important trading center.

◀ Because New York City was surrounded by water, shipping was important to the growth of the city. Ships carrying furs, crops, and other goods sailed from New York City to Europe and other British colonies like Connecticut and New Jersey. This painting shows New York City as it was around 1755.

New York Colonial Life

New York towns were built around meeting houses where church services and town meetings were held. Boys usually learned the jobs their fathers had learned. Girls were taught how to sew, cook, and make candles.

Most New York colonists were English and Dutch, but there were also many other groups, like Germans and Africans. The 1991 discovery of an old African burial ground is helping scientists and **historians** study how Africans lived in colonial New York. Most were slaves, but some were free men and women.

Because colonial leaders welcomed people from different backgrounds, people of many religions came to New York. Protestants, Catholics, and Jews all settled in the colony.

◀ The first schools that colonial boys and girls attended were called dame schools because they were taught by women, or dames, in their homes. Some larger towns had schools for older children, where most of the students were boys. Usually, only boys from wealthy families went on to college.

20

Food and Clothing

New York colonists ate **traditional** English foods like meat, cheese, and bread. They also enjoyed Native American foods like corn, beans, and pumpkins. Colonists made stews from meat and vegetables, and cooked the stews in a pot over an open fire.

Colonists' clothes were much like English clothing of that time. Women and girls wore long skirts or dresses over a **shift**. Men wore **frock coats**, shirts, and **breeches**. Clothes were made mostly of cotton and wool. Only wealthy people could afford expensive cloth like silk.

◀ This family picture was painted around 1772 by an artist named William Williams. It shows a wealthy British colonial family dressed in the clothing of the time. Lower Manhattan can be seen in the distance behind them.

Revolution!

England spent a lot of money to win the French and Indian War. The king of England could not afford to keep British soldiers in the colonies to prevent another war. He made the colonists help pay the expenses by taxing things like sugar, paper, cloth, and tea. The colonists thought this was unfair because they had no say in making the rules about the taxes. They joined together to fight the British.

In 1775, the **American Revolution** began. On July 4, 1776, colonial leaders signed the **Declaration of Independence**, which said that the colonies were free from English rule. A New Yorker named Robert Livingston helped to write this important American **document**. In 1783, the colonists won the war. New York City became the first capital of the new nation—the United States of America!

Glossary

Algonquian (al-GAHN-kwee-uhn) The name given to several groups of Native Americans in the northeast who spoke Algonquian languages.

American Revolution (uh-MAIR-uh-kuhn reh-vuh-LOO-shun) The war that the American colonists fought from 1775 to 1783 to win independence from England.

breeches (BREE-chuz) Loose pants that end just below the knee.

Declaration of Independence (deh-kluh-RAY-shun UV in-duh-PEN-duhns) A paper signed on July 4, 1776, in which the American colonies said that they were free from English rule.

document (DAH-kyoo-munt) Something printed or written that can be used as proof of facts.

frock coat (FRAHK KOTE) A coat with long sleeves that ends above the knee. Frock coats were worn by colonial boys and men.

historian (hih-STOR-ee-uhn) Someone who studies history.

Iroquois (EAR-uh-kwoy) The name given to several groups of Native Americans in the northeast who spoke Iroquois languages.

natural resource (NAH-chuh-ruhl REE-sohrs) Something found on the land or in the water that people can use, such as trees, fish, and coal.

profitable (PRAH-fuh-tuh-buhl) Providing income.

shift (SHIFT) A plain, lightweight garment worn under a dress.

surrender (suh-REHN-duhr) To give up.

traditional (truh-DIH-shuh-nuhl) The way something has been done or made by a group of people for a long time.

23

Index

Primary Source List

Cover. New Amsterdam on Manhattan Island. Lithograph, ca. 1800. Based on engraving by Thomas Doesburgh from Carel Allard's *Orbis habitabilis oppida et vestitus*, ca. 1700.

Page 4. Portrait of Peter Stuyvesant. Engraving, undated. Copy of portrait of Peter Stuyvesant, ca. 1650, in the New-York Historical Society.

Page 6. *Towne of Mannados or New Amsterdam*, 1664, in the British Library.

Page 8. Algonquian cooking fish. Hand-colored engraving by Theodor de Bry from Thomas Hariot's *A Briefe and True Report of the New Found Land of Virginia*, 1588. Based on watercolor by John White, 1585–1587.

Page 10. Title page from Daniel Denton's pamphlet *A Brief Description of New York*, 1670. Only twenty-one copies of the first edition are known to survive.

Page 12. *Carte des possessions angloises & françoises du continent de l'Amérique septentrionale*. Engraving by Thomas Kitchen, 1755. Map published by Jean Palairet.

Page 14. Page from account ledger of George Washington, 1754. In the George Washington Papers at the Library of Congress, Washington, D.C.

Page 15. South Barracks, Fort Ticonderoga. Built by French forces in 1755 and named Fort Carillon. Captured by British forces in 1759 and renamed Fort Ticonderoga. Cannon is an eighteenth-century howitzer.

Page 16. *View of New York City and New York Harbor*. Painting, ca. 1755. Now in the New-York Historical Society.

Page 20. *The William Denning Family*. Painting by William Williams, 1772.

Web Sites